# AMAZING SCIENCE
# AMAZING PLANTS

## Sally Hewitt

 Crabtree Publishing Company
www.crabtreebooks.com

## Crabtree Publishing Company

www.crabtreebooks.com

**Editors:** L. Michelle Nielsen, Michael Hodge
**Senior Editor:** Joyce Bentley
**Senior Design Manager:** Rosamund Saunders
**Designer:** Tall Tree

**Photo Credits:** Corbis: p. 3, p. 10, p. 11, p. 15; Paul Edmondson: p. 26; Andrew Brown/Ecoscene: p. 12; Nick Hawkes/Ecoscene: p. 21; Sally Morgan/Ecoscene: p. 19; Kjell Sandved/Ecoscene: p. 25; David Wootton/Ecoscene: p. 14; First Light/Getty Images: p. 22; Iconica/Getty Images: p. 13; Photographer's Choice/Getty Images: cover, p. 18; Photonica/Getty Images: p. 16, p. 17, p. 27; Stone/Getty Images: p. 20; Taxi/Getty Images: p. 23, p. 24; Bsip/Photo Library: p. 7; Christopher Talbot Frank/Photo Library: p. 9; Mark Hamblin/Photo Library: p. 8; Mode Images/Photo Library: p. 6

**Activity & illustrations:** Shakespeare Squared pp. 28-29.

**Cover:** A sunflower grows up toward the sunlight.

**Title page:** A wasp feeding on a flower.

**Library and Archives Canada Cataloguing in Publication**

Hewitt, Sally, 1949-
    Amazing plants / Sally Hewitt.

(Amazing science)
Includes index.
ISBN 978-0-7787-3614-1 (bound)
ISBN 978-0-7787-3628-8 (pbk.)

    1. Plants--Juvenile literature. 2. Botany--Juvenile literature.
I. Title. II. Series: Hewitt, Sally, 1949- . Amazing science.

QK49.H49 2007        j580        C2007-904311-9

**Library of Congress Cataloging-in-Publication Data**

Hewitt, Sally, 1949-
    Amazing plants / Sally Hewitt.
        p. cm. -- (Amazing science)
    Includes index.
    ISBN-13: 978-0-7787-3614-1 (rlb)
    ISBN-10: 0-7787-3614-8 (rlb)
    ISBN-13: 978-0-7787-3628-8 (pb)
    ISBN-10: 0-7787-3628-8 (pb)
    1. Plants--Juvenile literature. I. Title. II. Series.

QK49.H515 2008
580--dc22

                                        2007027469

## Crabtree Publishing Company

www.crabtreebooks.com        1-800-387-7650

**Published in Canada**
**Crabtree Publishing**
616 Welland Ave.
St. Catharines, Ontario
L2M 5V6

**Published in the United States**
**Crabtree Publishing**
PMB16A
350 Fifth Ave., Suite 3308
New York, NY 10118

Published by **CRABTREE PUBLISHING COMPANY**
Copyright © **2008**

# Contents

# Amazing plants

Giant sequoia trees are the tallest **plants** on Earth. They grow to over 295 feet (90 meters) tall and can weigh 2,205 tons (2,000 tons).

Plants are **alive**. They need **air**, **light**, and **water** to live and **grow**.

A plant can be as big as a tree or as small as a daisy.

A daisy is a kind of plant that grows **flowers**.

**YOUR TURN!**

*You are alive. Plants are alive. What other things are alive?*

**SCIENCE WORDS:** alive   grow   plant

7

# Where do plants grow?

Plants grow everywhere from mountains to under the sea. Many different types of plants can grow in one small forest.

Plants find ways of growing wherever they live on Earth, but they always need to find air, light, and water.

Cactus plants grow in deserts where there is plenty of light but very little water.

**YOUR TURN!**

*Find an area of a park or garden. How many different plants can you find growing around you?*

When it rains, cactus plants store water in their thick **stems**.

**SCIENCE WORDS:  air   light   water**

# Parts of a plant

Most parts of a plant grow above the ground, but **roots** grow under the soil. Roots can be the biggest part of a plant.

Every part of a plant does an important job. Roots suck up water.

The stem supports the plant. **Leaves** make food, and flowers are where **seeds** are made.

**YOUR TURN!**

*Pull up a weed and look carefully at the parts.*

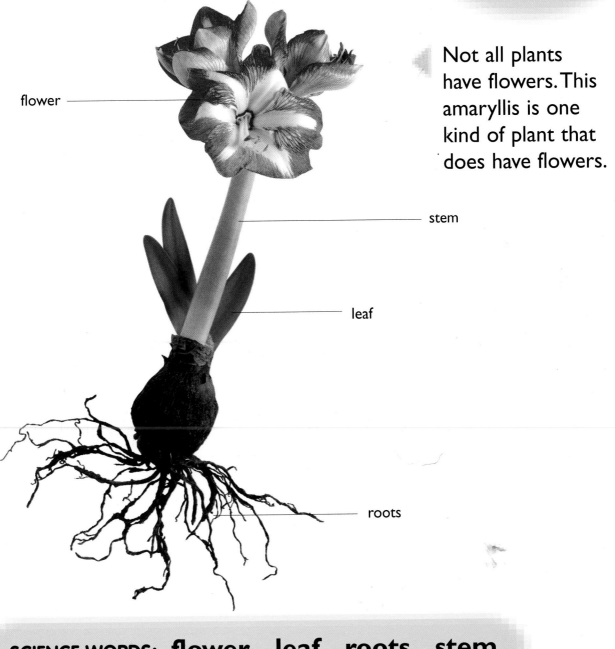

Not all plants have flowers. This amaryllis is one kind of plant that does have flowers.

flower

stem

leaf

roots

**SCIENCE WORDS: flower leaf roots stem**

# Sunlight

In the **rainforest,** smaller plants grow high up on the branches of trees so that they can be closer to **sunlight**.

Plants use energy from sunlight to make **food** in their leaves.

In the summer, some trees store the food that they make, and then they lose their leaves in the winter when there is less sunlight.

**YOUR TURN!**

*Put a potted plant in a dark place for several days. What happens to it?*

Some green leaves turn red and gold in autumn before they die in winter.

**SCIENCE WORDS:** **food   sunlight**

# Flowers

The rafflesia from Southeast Asia is the biggest flower in the world. Flies visit it because of its rotten smell.

Flowers are the part of a plant where seeds are made.

Flowers use a dust called **pollen** to make seeds. Pollen sticks to insects when they visit flowers for food.

**YOUR TURN!**

*On a sunny day, watch insects visit flowers for food. Look for pollen sticking to their legs and bodies.*

Insects carry pollen from flower to flower so new seeds can be made.

**SCIENCE WORDS:** **insect   pollen   seed**

# Fruit and seeds

A watermelon has red, juicy flesh and black seeds. It is the part of a plant called the **fruit**. It is yummy to eat!

When a flower dies, the fruit grows and falls to the ground. Fruit gives seeds the food that they need to grow into a new plant.

**Nuts** are seeds. Squirrels eat some nuts and bury others in the ground to eat later.

**YOUR TURN!**

Ask an adult to help you cut open some fruit. Find the seeds inside.

Some of the nuts that squirrels bury grow into trees.

**SCIENCE WORDS:** **fruit nut**

17

# Seedlings

A tall sunflower grows from a little striped seed. Inside the seed is everything that it needs to grow.

A seed grows into a new plant called a **seedling**.

The seedling grows into a plant that makes new seeds, and the **life cycle** starts again.

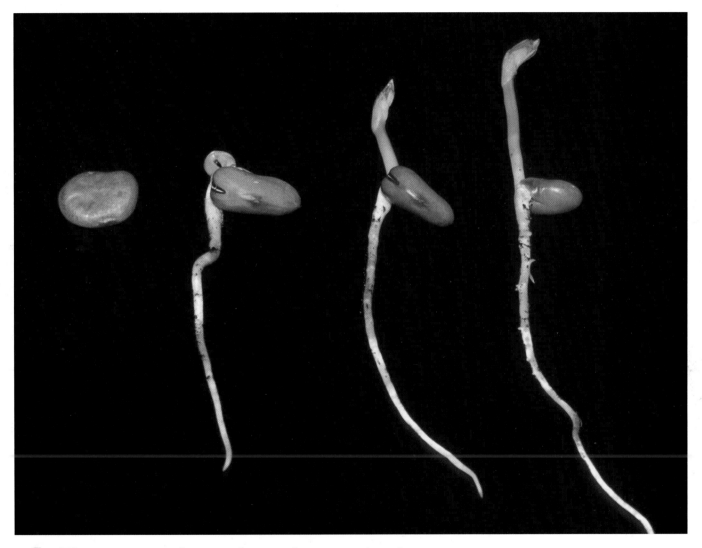

The picture above shows how a plant's roots and stem break out of the seed. These are the first stages in a plant's life cycle.

**SCIENCE WORDS:   life cycle  seedling**

# Plants to eat

Fields of golden **wheat** stretch as far as the eye can see. Wheat is a grass. It is one of the many plants that people eat.

Wheat seeds, called **grain**, are ground into flour to make bread and pasta.

The food that we eat comes from different parts of plants. Carrots are roots. Celery stalks are stems. Lettuces are leaves, and broccoli are flowers.

The parts of plants that we eat are called vegetables or fruit.

**YOUR TURN!**

*What is your favourite vegetable? What part of a plant is it?*

**SCIENCE WORDS:  grain   wheat**

# Useful plants

In some countries, trees are cut down for their **wood**. These wood logs are floating down river toward a saw mill.

Wood is cut at saw mills and then used to make furniture and paper.

Cotton for making clothes and rubber for making tires also come from plants.

**YOUR TURN!**

*Find things at home made from plants. What plants are they made from?*

Medicine made from plants helps make people better when they are sick.

**SCIENCE WORDS:  make  wood**

# Extraordinary plants

Like all plants, Venus flytraps need air, water, and light to grow, but they also eat flies, other **insects**, and spiders!

Venus flytraps close their leaves, like jaws, around insects and spiders that land on them.

Plants called "lithops" mimic, or look like, pebbles, which **protects** them from hungry animals.

**YOUR TURN!**

*How else do plants protect themselves from being eaten?*

Lithops are hard to spot on pebbly ground.

**SCIENCE WORDS: mimic protect**

# Underwater plants

**Underwater** plants have long, bendy stems that sway in flowing water. Sea kelp clings tightly to rocks underwater.

Underwater plants need sunlight and **oxygen** to grow.

Bubbles of oxygen fill the water, and the plants make food from sunlight.

**YOUR TURN!**

Look for plants that grow up walls and trees. Why do you think they have long bendy stems?

Underwater plants and animals all need oxygen to live and grow.

**SCIENCE WORDS:** **oxygen** **underwater**

# The thirsty celery

Do this activity to see how important water is to plants, including plants that you eat.

## What you need
- wilted celery stalk with leaves
- glass jar
- water
- pencil
- paper
- scissors
- food coloring

1. Use a wilted celery stalk for this activity. (A wilted celery stalk is probably a few days or a week old and not crisp anymore.) Cut about an inch (2.5 cm) off of the end of the stalk that does not have the leaves.

2. Fill the jar about halfway with water. Squeeze four or five drops of food coloring into the water and stir.

**3.** Place the celery into the colored water. Make sure that the cut end is down and that the leaves are not in the water. Set your jar someplace where it will not be disturbed.

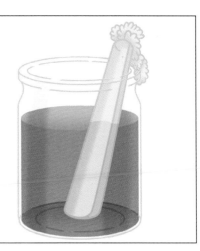

**4.** Come back the next day and look at your celery stalk. What has happened? How has it changed? Do the leaves look different? Record your observations on a piece of paper.

## What happened:

Water is important to plants. Without water, plants cannot survive. Your piece of celery that started as a wilted and weak plant is now strong. This is because it now has enough water to survive. Also, what do you see when you look at the leaves? The tips of the leaves are now the same color as the food coloring! This is because plants have parts that are similar to the veins in your body. These parts carry water and nutrients to the entire plant, including the leaves, to make them healthy and strong. That is why the grocery store always sprays vegetables with water!

# Glossary

**air**   An invisible gas that people, animals, and plants need to live.

**alive**   Things that are alive move, grow, eat and drink. A plant is alive and so are you.

**flower**   The part of a plant where seeds are made.

**food**   The things that animals and plants take in for life and growth.

**fruit**   The part of a plant that protects the seeds.

**grain**   A grain is a small, hard seed.

**grow**   To grow is to get bigger and to change. A seed becomes a seedling, then a plant.

**insect**   A small animal that has three pairs of legs, a body, a head, and often wings.

**leaves**   The part of a plant that makes food.

**life cycle**   The growing stages of an animal or plant.

**light**   Rays from the sun, a flashlight, or a lamp that allow us to see.

**Nut**   A nut is a kind of seed.

**oxygen**   A gas in the air. Animals and plants need oxygen to live.

**plant**   A living thing that grows on Earth or in water and usually has green leaves.

**pollen**   Yellow powder made by flowers.

**protect**   To protect something is to stop it from being harmed.

**rainforests**   Forests in warm areas that get a lot of rain and where many types of plants grow.

**root**   The part of a plant that grows under ground and sucks up water.

**seed**   The part of a plant from which a new plant grows.

**seedling**   A new, young plant.

**stem**   The part of a plant from which flowers and leaves grow.

**sunlight**   Light from the Sun. Plants make their food from sunlight.

**underwater**   Underwater plants grow and live completely under water.

**water**   A clear liquid that animals and plants take in for life and growth.

**wheat**   A kind of grass. We make bread from grains of wheat.

**wood**   Wood comes from plants called a trees. We use it to make furniture and paper.

# Index

Printed in the USA